Y0-BLE-559

ROSTRAVER PUBLIC LIBRARY

700 PLAZA DRIVE
BELLE VERNON, PA 15012
724-379-5511

CHILDHOOD FEARS AND ANXIETIES

FAMILY FEARS

CHILDHOOD FEARS AND ANXIETIES

Anxiety and Fear in Daily Life

Catastrophes

Crime and Terrorism

Family Fears

Medical Fears

Nighttime Fears

Phobias

School Fears

Separation Anxiety

Social Fears

Symptoms and Treatments of Anxiety Disorders

CHILDHOOD FEARS
AND ANXIETIES

FAMILY FEARS

H.W. POOLE

SERIES CONSULTANT
ANNE S. WALTERS, Ph.D.
Emma Pendleton Bradley Hospital

Warren Alpert Medical School of
Brown University

MASON CREST

Mason Crest
450 Parkway Drive, Suite D
Broomall, PA 19008
www.masoncrest.com

© 2018 by Mason Crest, an imprint of National Highlights, Inc. All rights reserved. No part of this publication may be reproduced or transmitted in any form or by any means, electronic or mechanical, including photocopying, recording, taping, or any information storage and retrieval system, without permission from the publisher.

MTM Publishing, Inc.
435 West 23rd Street, #8C
New York, NY 10011
www.mtmpublishing.com

President: Valerie Tomaselli
Vice President, Book Development: Hilary Poole
Designer: Annemarie Redmond
Copyeditor: Peter Jaskowiak
Editorial Assistant: Leigh Eron

Series ISBN: 978-1-4222-3721-2
Hardback ISBN: 978-1-4222-3725-0
E-Book ISBN: 978-1-4222-8058-4

Library of Congress Cataloging-in-Publication Data
Names: Poole, Hilary W., author.
Title: Family fears / by H.W. Poole; Series Consultant: Anne S. Walters, Ph.D.
Description: Broomall, PA : Mason Crest, [2018] | Series: Childhood fears and anxieties | Includes index.
Identifiers: LCCN 2017000510 (print) | LCCN 2017017656 (ebook) | ISBN 9781422280584 (ebook) | ISBN 9781422237250 (hardback: alk. paper)
Subjects: LCSH: Families—Juvenile literature. | Anxiety in children—Juvenile literature.
Classification: LCC HQ744 (ebook) | LCC HQ744 .P559 2018 (print) | DDC 306.85—dc23
LC record available at https://lccn.loc.gov/2017000510

Printed and bound in the United States of America.

First printing
9 8 7 6 5 4 3 2 1

QR CODES AND LINKS TO THIRD PARTY CONTENT
You may gain access to certain third party content ("Third Party Sites") by scanning and using the QR Codes that appear in this publication (the "QR Codes"). We do not operate or control in any respect any information, products or services on such Third Party Sites linked to by us via the QR Codes included in this publication and we assume no responsibility for any materials you may access using the QR Codes. Your use of the QR Codes may be subject to terms, limitations, or restrictions set forth in the applicable terms of use or otherwise established by the owners of the Third Party Sites. Our linking to such Third Party Sites via the QR Codes does not imply an endorsement or sponsorship of such Third Party Sites, or the information, products or services offered on or through the Third Party Sites, nor does it imply an endorsement or sponsorship of this publication by the owners of such Third Party Sites.

TABLE OF CONTENTS

Series Introduction 6
Chapter One: Family Troubles 9
Chapter Two: Separation and Divorce 15
Chapter Three: Moving 29
Chapter Four: Death 37
Further Reading 44
Series Glossary 45
Index 47
About the Advisor 48
About the Author 48
Photo Credits 48

Key Icons to Look for:

Words to Understand: These words with their easy-to-understand definitions will increase the reader's understanding of the text, while building vocabulary skills.

Sidebars: This boxed material within the main text allows readers to build knowledge, gain insights, explore possibilities, and broaden their perspectives by weaving together additional information to provide realistic and holistic perspectives.

Educational Videos: Readers can view videos by scanning our QR codes, which will provide them with additional educational content to supplement the text. Examples include news coverage, moments in history, speeches, iconic sports moments, and much more.

Text-Dependent Questions: These questions send the reader back to the text for more careful attention to the evidence presented there.

Research Projects: Readers are pointed toward areas of further inquiry connected to each chapter. Suggestions are provided for projects that encourage deeper research and analysis.

Series Glossary of Key Terms: This back-of-the-book glossary contains terminology used throughout the series. Words found here increase the reader's ability to read and comprehend higher-level books and articles in this field.

SERIES INTRODUCTION

Who among us does not have memories of an intense childhood fear? Fears and anxieties are a part of *every* childhood. Indeed, these fears are fodder for urban legends and campfire tales alike. And while the details of these legends and tales change over time, they generally have at their base predictable childhood terrors such as darkness, separation from caretakers, or bodily injury.

We know that fear has an evolutionary component. Infants are helpless, and, compared to other mammals, humans have a very long developmental period. Fear ensures that curious children will stay close to caretakers, making them less likely to be exposed to danger. This means that childhood fears are adaptive, making us more likely to survive, and even thrive, as a species.

Unfortunately, there comes a point when fear and anxiety cease to be useful. This is especially problematic today, for there has been a startling increase in anxiety among children and adolescents. In fact, 25 percent of 13- to 18-year-olds now have mild to moderate anxiety, and the *median* age of onset for anxiety disorders is just 11 years old.

Why might this be? Some say that the contemporary United States is a nation preoccupied with risk, and it is certainly possible that our children are absorbing this preoccupation as well. Certainly, our exposure to potential threats has never been greater. We see graphic images via the media and have more immediate news of all forms of disaster. This can lead our children to feel more vulnerable, and it may increase the likelihood that they respond with fear. If children based their fear on the news that they see on Facebook or on TV, they would dramatically overestimate the likelihood of terrible things happening.

As parents or teachers, what do we do about fear? As in other areas of life, we provide our children with guidance and education on a daily basis. We teach them about the signs and feelings of fear. We discuss and normalize typical fear reactions, and support them in tackling difficult situations despite fear. We explain—and demonstrate by example—how to identify "negative thinking traps" and generate positive coping thoughts instead.

But to do so effectively, we might need to challenge some of our own assumptions about fear. Adults often assume that they must protect their children from fear and help them to avoid scary situations, when sometimes the best course is for the child to face the fear and conquer it. This is counterintuitive for many adults: after all, isn't it our job to reassure our children and help them feel better? Yes, of course! Except when it isn't. Sometimes they need us to help them confront their fears and move forward anyway.

That's where these volumes come in. When it comes to fear, balanced information is critical. Learning about fear as it relates to many different areas can help us to help our children remember that although you don't choose whether to be afraid, you do choose how to handle it. These volumes explore the world of childhood fears, seeking to answer important questions: How much is too much? And how can fear be positive, functioning to mobilize us in the face of danger?

Fear gives us the opportunity to step up and respond with courage and resilience. It pushes us to expand our sphere of functioning to areas that might feel unfamiliar or risky. When we are a little nervous or afraid, we tend to prepare a little more, look for more information, ask more questions—and all of this can function to help us expand the boundaries of our lives in a positive direction. So, while fear might *feel* unpleasant, there is no doubt that it can have a positive outcome.

Let's teach our children that.

—Anne Walters, Ph.D.
Chief Psychologist, Emma Pendleton Bradley Hospital
Clinical Associate Professor,
Alpert Medical School of Brown University

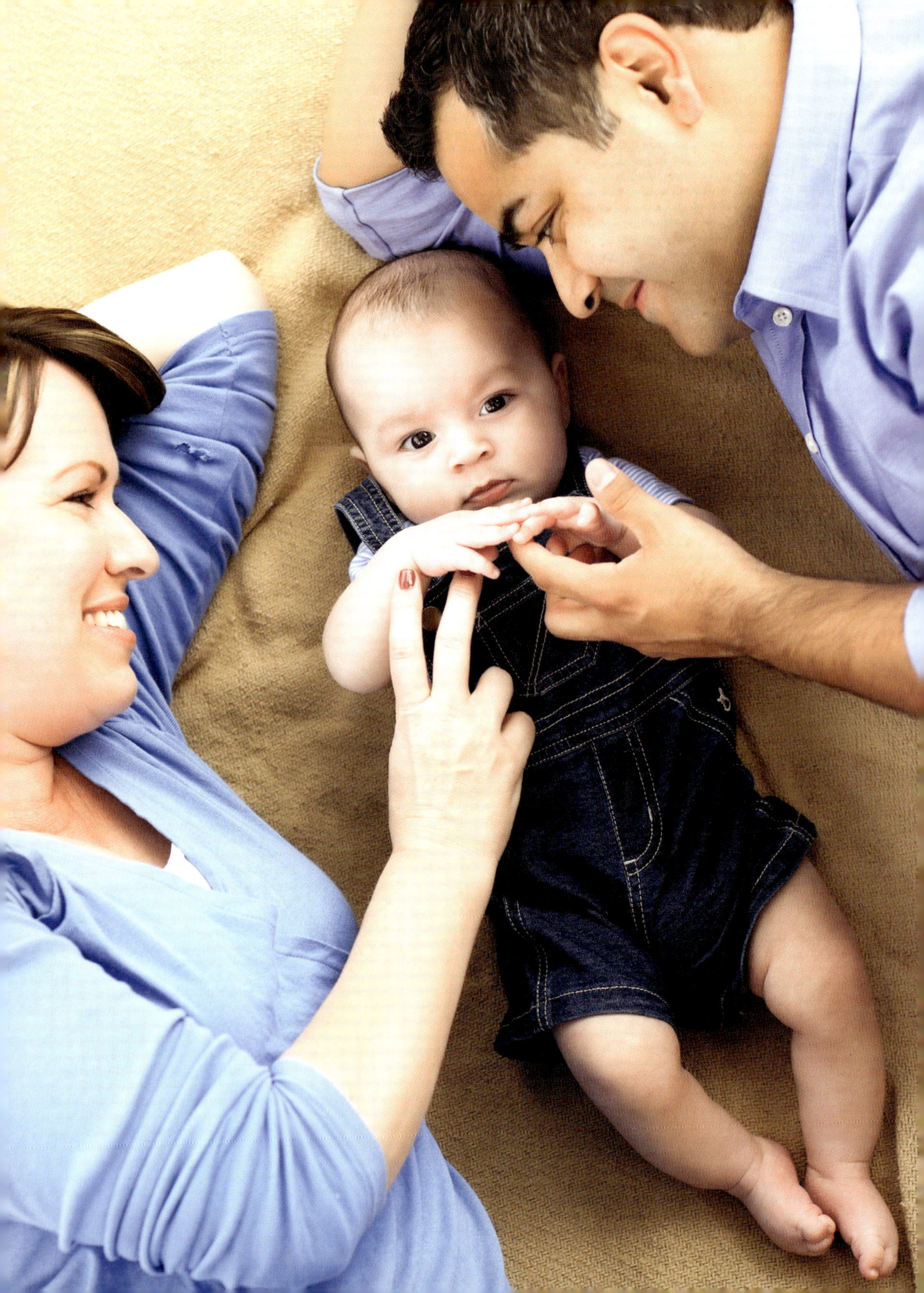

CHAPTER ONE

FAMILY TROUBLES

When babies are born, they are extremely **vulnerable**. Unlike most other animals, newborn humans can't take care of themselves at all. The process that we call "growing up" is basically a series of steps toward becoming more and more independent. But even middle-school kids are pretty dependent on the adults around them for food, shelter, and education.

Consequently, it's easy to understand why the family is the center of most kids' lives. And it also makes sense that a lot of the fears and anxieties that kids have are related to their families. When you are dependent on others for your own survival, it's natural to worry about the safety of those people. Even very little kids understand, at least on a **subconscious** level, that the fate of their parents is intertwined with their own.

WORDS TO UNDERSTAND

deployment: the movement of troops into a particular area.

deportation: the act of forcing a noncitizen to leave a country.

incarceration: being confined in prison.

subconscious: the part of your mind you are not always aware of, or the things you are thinking about beneath your daily thoughts.

vulnerable: easily harmed or attacked.

EDUCATIONAL VIDEO

Check out this video with advice about dealing with family anxiety.

WHAT MIGHT HAPPEN

Anxiety about your family is not like anxiety about a monster in your closet. I can promise you without even looking that there is no monster in your closet. But the same thing can't be said when it comes to family fears. After all, bad things do happen. Some parents do get sick, some couples do get divorced, and so on. But just because those things happen, that does not mean that they will happen to you. In fact, statistics suggest that these events are fairly unlikely. Still, whatever you fear feels plenty real to you, even if you know it's not likely to happen.

It can be upsetting and even scary when your family isn't getting along.

FAMILY TROUBLES

TYPES OF FEARS

There are lots of possible family-related fears. Here are some examples:
- illness, injury, or death of a parent
- illness, injury, or death of a sibling
- parents fighting
- divorce
- moving
- loss of home (being homeless)
- arrest or **incarceration** of parent
- **deployment** of parent (if the parent is in the military)
- **deportation** of parent (if the parent is an immigrant)

That's a lot of stuff to worry about! We can't cover all of it in one book, but we will look at some of the most common family-related fears.

A march in support of immigration reform in Los Angeles. Living under the threat of deportation is tough on kids, who may constantly worry that their families could get broken up.

Being afraid from time to time is totally normal. There will always be a certain level of uncertainty in life—we can't know what tomorrow or next week

FAMILY FEARS

will bring, after all. The trick is to acknowledge your concerns without letting them take charge of you.

PARENTS AND CAREGIVERS

This book is going to talk a lot about the main components of a typical family: parents and children. But it's important to recognize that not all families look the same.

Around 5 percent of American kids don't live with their parents. Five percent might sound like a small amount, but did you know that there are nearly 74 million Americans under the age of 18? So 5 percent is still a lot of people! The majority of these kids live with a grandparent or other member of their

More than 2.5 million grandparents are the primary caregivers for their grandchildren.

FAMILY TROUBLES

extended family. Others are in foster care: more than 600,000 kids spend at least some time in foster care at some point in a given year.

Kids who don't live with their parents still feel all the same anxieties as kids who do. In fact, kids who don't live with their parents often feel *more* anxiety than other kids, precisely because they don't live with their parents. They have experienced family problems firsthand, and they may worry that a loss could happen again.

Even though this book will use the word *parents* a lot, the issues being discussed apply to all kids and the adults who care for them. In the context of this book, it doesn't matter whether you are related to your caregiver or not. The point is, you depend on your caregiver, and the thought that something bad could happen might make you anxious. That's normal. This book will look more closely at some family fears and offer suggestions about what to do.

RESEARCH PROJECT

Survey as many people as you can about what family fears they have now or had when they were younger. Ask people to rate how worried they were on a scale from 1 to 10. Tally your results—what are the most common fears?

TEXT-DEPENDENT QUESTIONS

1. Why do kids worry about the safety of their parents?
2. What are some of the bad things that might happen to parents?
3. What percentage of American kids live with someone other than their parent?

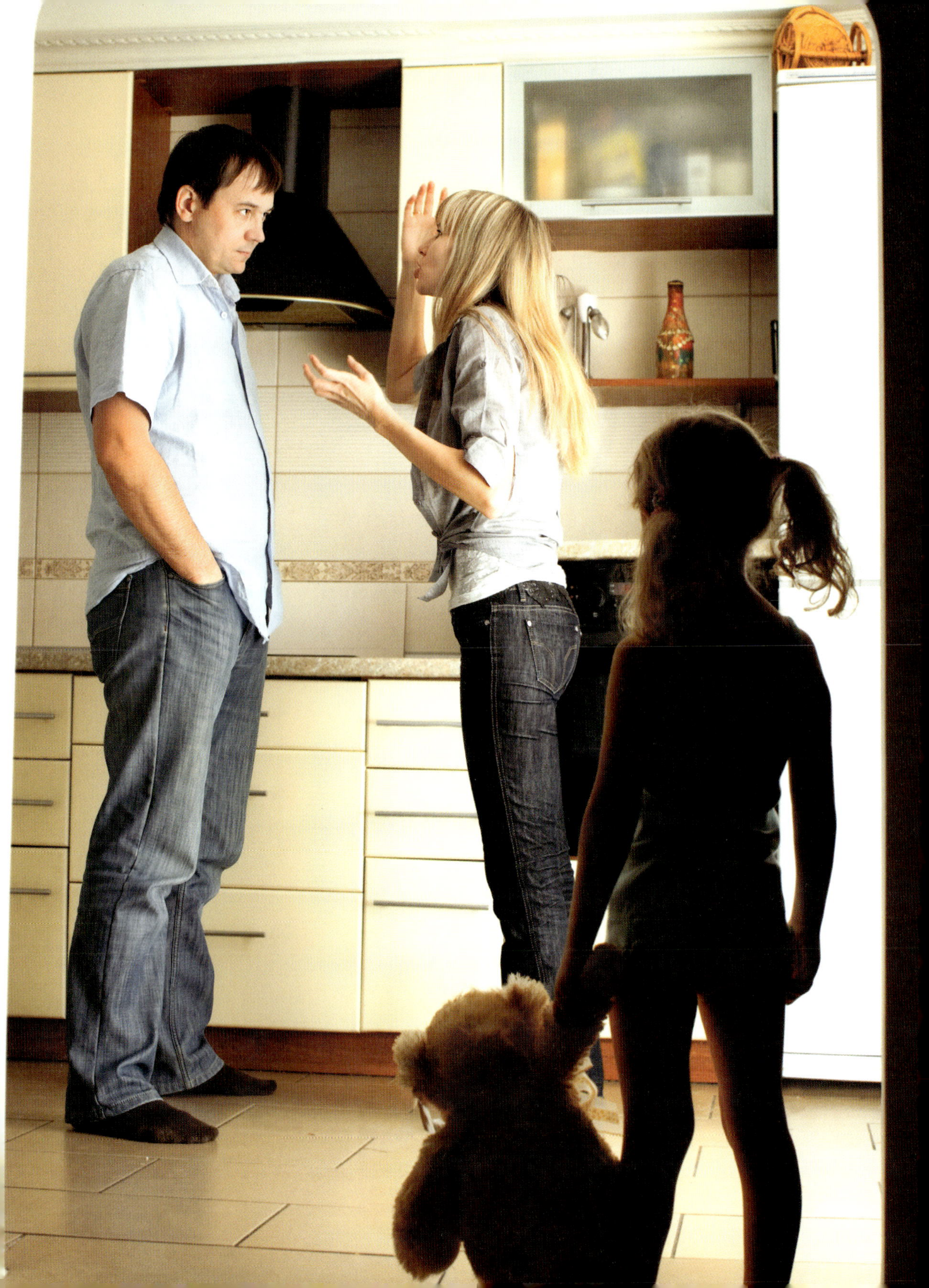

CHAPTER TWO

SEPARATION AND DIVORCE

When two people get married, they promise to stick together forever, no matter what. And when people recite those vows, they tend to mean them. Unfortunately, the good intentions that people have on their wedding days don't always result in living "happily ever after." Sometimes married couples find that they can't get along anymore, or that they are making each other very unhappy. In those situations, they may choose to get a divorce.

WHAT IS A DIVORCE?

You've probably seen weddings on television or in movies—you may even have been to one or two yourself. Usually, people get all dressed up, there is a ceremony, and then there is a big party with cake and presents. But marriage is more than a party—it actually has a very specific legal meaning.

Under the law, two people who are married are viewed as one unit. They have the right to pay their

WORDS TO UNDERSTAND

custody: the right to be in charge of and care for someone or something.

permissive: allowing for a large amount of freedom.

spouse: husband or wife.

A wedding is more than just a party; it unites two people under the law.

taxes together, for example. They can easily buy property together. They can get loans or apply for credit cards in one another's names. If one half of the couple gets sick, the **spouse** can make important medical decisions on the other person's behalf. If one half of the couple is a citizen of the United States but the other is not, the spouse who is not a citizen gets special immigration privileges. Married couples even get special treatment in court: one spouse can't be forced to give evidence against the other. All these benefits spring from the basic idea that a married couple is one unit rather than two separate individuals.

A divorce legally separates two married people. Once two people are divorced, they are no longer viewed as being a unit under the law. In addition, all their belongings have to be divided between them.

SEPARATIONS

A middle step between marriage and divorce is called *separation*. There are a couple of different types of separation, and a few different reasons why they happen.

In a "trial separation," a married couple will live apart for a period of time as they try and make up their minds about whether to stay married or not. In a "legal separation," the court system gets involved. A legally binding document is created, and the couple agrees on how they are going to handle certain aspects of their relationship, such as financial support and child custody. Some states require that couples try some form of separation before they can get a divorce.

Sometimes even happy couples end up separated. A spouse might have to travel far away for work, for example. Similarly, military families may be separated during a spouse's deployment. Or if a spouse is convicted of a crime, he or she may have to spend time in prison or jail.

These separations are different from the trial and legal separations mentioned above because they are imposed by outside circumstances. They aren't a reflection of how the two people feel about one another.

Some separations have nothing to do with marriage problems. But that doesn't make them easier to live through.

FAMILY FEARS

Let's say that a married couple owns two cars—the husband drives one car to his job, and the wife drives the other car to her job. Legally, both cars might be owned by both people. But in daily life, one of the cars "belongs" to the husband and one to the wife. If the couple divorces, figuring out who keeps which car will therefore be pretty simple.

But dividing up other possessions is not always so straightforward. For instance, if that same couple owns a house, a decision will need to be made about how to share it in a fair way. The house might be sold, and the money from the sale divided equally. Or maybe one person will keep the house and the other spouse will get some other possession in return. Any decision is okay, as long as both people agree to it. Reaching an agreement can be tough sometimes, however, since people who are getting divorced may not be getting along very well. Certain lawyers and counselors specialize in figuring out these problems.

If a divorcing couple has kids, decisions also must made to determine who will care for them. This is called **custody**, and there are two types—legal and physical. The person with physical custody is the one who lives with the kids and is responsible for their daily care. Legal custody, on the other hand, relates to who makes decisions for the kids (such as where they live and where they go to school) until they turn 18.

When parents get divorced, it's common for one parent to have physical custody, while both parents

SEPARATION AND DIVORCE

share legal custody. The parent who does not have physical custody might have visitation rights, meaning that he or she gets to see their kid(s) at certain periods of time. However, there is no single "correct" way to handle custody after a divorce. All families are different, and there are all kinds of compromises that can be worked out.

IS IT GOING TO HAPPEN TO ME?

You might have heard somebody say that "half of all marriages end in divorce." Here's some good news: this is actually not true.

For a long time, it was actually pretty difficult to get a divorce. Simply being unhappy was not considered

Sometimes one divorced parent has primary custody, while the other has visitation rights.

enough of a reason to end a marriage. There had to be some other, very specific reason, and either the husband or the wife had to admit to being legally "at fault" for the marriage ending. But in the 1970s, a new type of divorce became available, called "no-fault" divorce. That's when two people can decide to end their marriage without giving any specific reason why. When no-fault divorce became common, there was an increase in divorce rates for a while. The belief that half of all marriages end up in divorce may come from that era.

However, rates of divorce have actually dropped a great deal in the 21st century. The annual divorce rate in the United States is 3.2 per 1,000 people. In other words, if you were to watch 1,000 average Americans for a year, roughly three of those people would get a divorce by the end of December that year. So if you are wondering if a divorce is going to happen to your family, the statistics tell us that the answer is a definite *maybe, but probably not*.

DEALING WITH DIVORCE FEARS

Our society has high expectations about what a "good" marriage is supposed to look like. Married couples are supposed to be best friends, helpful partners, excellent parents, *and* lovey-dovey like boyfriends and girlfriends, all at the same time. That's a tall order, and most humans can't be great at all those things all the time. It's basically inevitable

SEPARATION AND DIVORCE

IF HOME ISN'T SAFE

A lot of troubled marriages involve two mismatched people who can't get along. It's sad when marriages break up, but most of the time everybody means well. Other times, the trouble is more serious.

Some parents struggle with drugs and alcohol, and their behavior can make life scary for their kids. Some parents have mental health problems. Sometimes there is physical abuse in the home. These situations are more serious, and they can't be handled in a short book like this one. But if you feel unsafe in your home, it is important to find someone who can help you. If you can, talk to a trusted adult—it could be a teacher or coach, someone from church, or a member of your extended family.

If there's nobody in your life who seems to fit the bill, here are some national organizations that want to help:
- National Child Abuse Hotline: 1-800-4-A-Child (1-800-422-4453); online: https://www.childhelp.org/hotline.
- National Sexual Assault Hotline: 1-800-656-HOPE (1-800-656-4673); online: https://hotline.rainn.org/online.

that, at one time or another, one spouse will disappoint or upset the other one.

All couples argue sometimes—how much depends on their personalities. Some couples argue frequently, while others tend to avoid conflict as much as they can. So just because you hear your parents argue, that does not mean a divorce is in your future. Yes, married people fight—but they also make up. In fact, sometimes arguments are the way couples work through their problems.

FAMILY FEARS

If you are concerned about your parents, try to discuss your worries with them.

If you are worried about your parents splitting up, the best thing to do is talk to them about it. How and when to have this conversation depends on your specific family situation. You might want to talk to just one parent at first. Or you could ask them both to sit down with you. If you don't feel comfortable bringing this up with your parents, consider if there is another adult in your life—such as another relative, someone from church, a coach, or a teacher—who you could talk to. Talking about the situation will do two good things: first, talking over your feelings is

SEPARATION AND DIVORCE

going to make you feel better; second, you might be able to make some positive change in your family.

This advice is easy to give but not always easy to follow. Initiating a conversation about problems in a relationship is one of the most difficult things to do. Adults included! It can be very hard to start a discussion about our feelings or worries. It's natural to want to pretend problems do not exist, or to hope they will just go away on their own. That very rarely happens, unfortunately. So although it may be hard, talking openly about your fears is the first step toward feeling better.

The truth is, parents often forget that when they aren't getting along, their kids notice. For instance, parents might wait until the kids are in bed to have an argument, not realizing that the whole discussion can be heard through the walls of the bedroom. Or sometimes people get grumpy and kind of "pick on" each other—criticizing little tiny things, or even making fun of each other in a mean way. Parents usually assume their kids aren't paying attention to those signals, but they are usually wrong. Adults may tell themselves that they are "acting normal," but their kids see right through it. Parents sometimes need a reminder about how their behavior affects their kids.

This is why it's important to be honest about your worries. Your parents may have no idea that they are upsetting you. If you talk to them about it, you might find that they can reassure you. It might be that other difficult things are happening in

EDUCATIONAL VIDEO

Check out this video where kids talk honestly about their feelings when their parents got divorced.

FAMILY FEARS

In the heat of an argument, it's easy for parents to forget that someone might be listening.

parents' lives that are causing the arguments. There might be disagreements about money, for instance, or problems with work.

IT HAPPENED TO ME

Unfortunately, it's also possible that the arguments *are* related to your parents' marriage. Every year, more than a million kids in the United States have to cope with their parents getting a divorce. What do you do if that happens?

Let's cover the easy part first: *it is not your fault*. Kids almost always want to blame themselves when

SEPARATION AND DIVORCE

their parents split up. They wonder things like, "maybe if I had behaved better, my parents would still be married," or "maybe if I had gotten better grades, my parents would still be married." No and no. Divorce is not ever the kids' fault.

Here's the hard part. When parents break up, it's common for kids to feel split down the middle. Most of the time, kids love both their parents equally, and when a divorce happens, kids feel like they have to pick a side. There are some very sad situations where, in fact, you might be better off with one parent than the other (see box on page 21). But most of the time, divorces happen between people who just can't get along. There is no reason why you, as the kid, should end up in the middle. You have a right to a good relationship with *both* your parents. It is their job to make that possible, even if they don't want to be married to each other anymore.

The first year after a divorce can be very hard on everybody involved. Somebody usually has to move—and sometimes everybody has to find a new place to live. There is stress about visiting rights and custody. Some divorced parents become overprotective—they feel that they failed at marriage, so they want to be "perfect" in every other way. Other parents become very **permissive**—they feel guilty about the divorce and want to make it up to their kids with gifts or trips.

As the one stuck in the middle, you might feel angry at your parents or worried about the future. Kids get their sense of security from their parents. When parents split up, that sense of security is destroyed, at least for a while. There are practical issues, too. When parents share custody, for example, kids have to get used to living part-time in different houses. It's really important for parents to put aside their personal differences and try to help their kids adjust.

Counseling is a really good idea in these situations. You have a right to your own feelings, and it can be helpful to talk with someone who is trained in working through painful situations. Counselors will also have advice for your parents. In fact, they will have suggestions about how to help the whole family adjust to the new reality.

This may be hard to believe when the divorce is happening, but, in time, things really can be okay. In fact, researchers have studied the long-term

Counseling can help families work on problems and understand each other better.

SEPARATION AND DIVORCE

impacts of divorce on kids. They looked at things like success in school, whether or not the kids get into trouble frequently, and the kids' overall attitudes about themselves and others. Overall, they found only minor differences between kids whose parents were divorced and those whose parents weren't. The researchers concluded that while divorce is hard on kids in the short term, the majority of kids turn out just fine in the long run.

Here's a funny thing about human nature. Situations that seem difficult or even impossible to deal with at first can become second-nature over time. For example, lots of families get used to dealing with shared custody; it might seem complicated or painful at first, but it becomes routine after a while. Many kids find that after some time has passed, their parents are happier apart than they were when they were together and fighting all the time. The most important thing is to ask for help when you need it, and to keep asking if you need to.

RESEARCH PROJECT

Create a pamphlet with advice for kids about how to cope with divorce. Gather advice from this book (including the Further Reading suggestions), and find your own online and at the library.

TEXT-DEPENDENT QUESTIONS

1. What are some of the legal benefits of married couples?

2. What are some types of separation? How are they different from each other?

3. Name two possible benefits of talking to your parents about your worries.

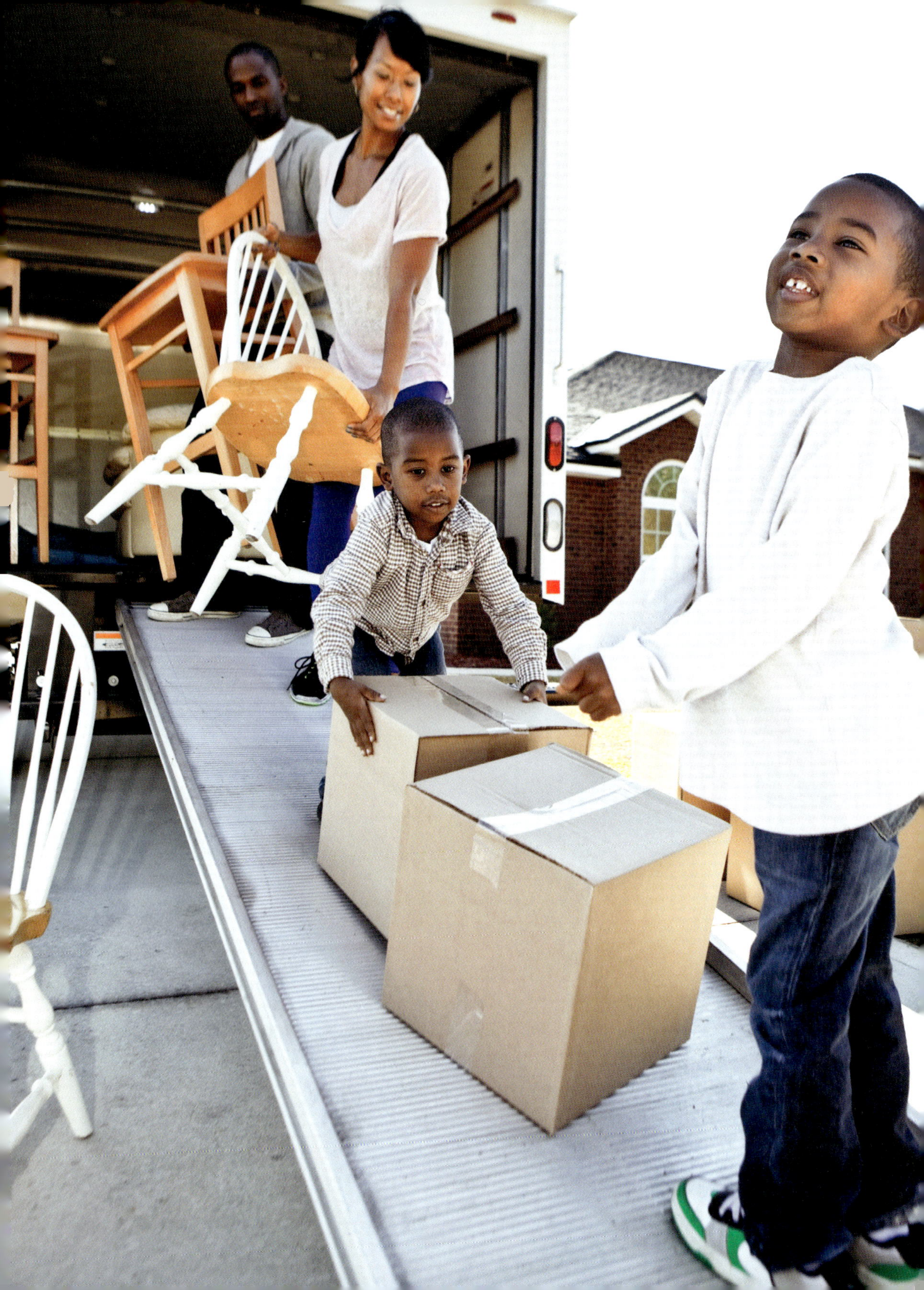

CHAPTER THREE

MOVING

Living through a divorce can make kids feel like their whole lives have been turned upside down. But that's not the only event that can cause uncertainty. Sometimes it's not the relationships in your life that change, but the location.

About 14 percent of Americans move in any given year. Of course, that number is a bit misleading, because it includes all Americans—from college kids leaving home for the first time, to newly married couples buying their first home, to elderly people moving into retirement communities. So it might be more helpful to talk about a more specific number: the average American will have moved twice by the time he or she turns 18.

WHY MOVE?

There are almost as many reasons to move as there are people who do it. The last chapter mentioned one reason to move: divorce. Another reason is employment—a parent might get transferred from an office in one city or state to an

WORDS TO UNDERSTAND

shelter: here, a temporary place for homeless people to stay.

upheaval: a period of great change or uncertainty.

FAMILY FEARS

Moving day is exciting, but it can bring a lot of anxiety as well.

office in another. Sometimes people move because they are searching for new jobs entirely.

Other times, families need a different sort of house. Their current house might be too expensive, or a new baby might mean the current house is too small. Or the neighborhood where they live might not be right for them anymore. For instance, some families move when kids are in middle school, because they are hoping that their children can attend a different high school somewhere else.

MOVING

LOSING HOME

Sometimes people leave their homes not because they want to, but because they have no other option. About 1 in 30 American kids experience homelessness in a given year.

Many of these kids don't look like our traditional picture of a "homeless person." About three-quarters of kids who are technically homeless are doing what's called "doubling up," meaning that they are staying with friends or family. A far smaller percentage of kids stay in **shelters**, and only a tiny sliver are completely "unsheltered," meaning that they live outside or in cars.

But whether you are sleeping in a car or on a friend's couch, being homeless adds huge amounts of uncertainty and anxiety to daily life. Going to school at all may seem difficult, and actually doing well at school might feel like an impossible dream. But most communities and schools have programs to assist homeless kids. And there is almost certainly at least one teacher at your school—and probably more—who would gladly help you.

Lots of kids keep their homelessness secret from their friends and teachers because they are embarrassed. That's totally natural. But try to ignore those feelings and ask for help anyway. Remember, homelessness is not your fault! It is important that you not let shame about your living situation prevent you from getting the assistance you need and deserve.

Another aspect of moving that varies a lot is the distance of the move. If your family moves from one apartment or house to another in the same area, the disruption in your life will be fairly small. You will have a new bedroom, of course, and you'll take a new route to school. But if you

EDUCATIONAL VIDEO

Check out this video with advice about moving to a new school.

Visiting your new school before a move can help reduce anxiety.

are staying in more-or-less the same community, life will probably not change very drastically.

On the other hand, if you move to a new city, state, or even a new country, you may be in for some pretty serious **upheaval**. The many changes that long-distance moves entail can cause large amounts of anxiety for some kids.

COPING WITH MOVING

If your family is planning a move and you feel anxious, information is your best weapon. The scariest parts of life tend to involve the unknown. Find out as much as you can about the new neighborhood you'll be moving to.

If your new location is close enough, try to visit at least once before the big day. Seeing the new place with your own eyes will make the move more concrete for you. If your new home is too far away for you to visit, ask your parents to show you pictures. Take advantage of all the information available on the Internet, too. Go to Google Maps and type in your new address, and you will probably find pictures of your street and even your house. Being able to picture your new neighborhood will help reduce anxiety.

While you are doing online research on your new community, you can try to find out what kinds of things people like to do there. Are there special events like parades or concerts? Is there a nice park

MOVING

FAMILY FEARS

or a zoo or an amusement park nearby? Do people like to ski, hike, or go to the beach? You can almost always find something intriguing if you look. This will help you have more to look forward to when you become a member of your new community.

But before you get there, you will have to say goodbye. In many ways, this is the hardest part of moving. If you are only moving a short distance, make plans to stay in touch with your friends. For instance, you might ask your parents to help you set up a visit from your old friends at your new house.

Even if you are moving far away, the Internet provides opportunities to stay in touch, such as e-mailing, texting, and video chatting. You may

Technology can help you stay in touch with people who are far away.

also be able to stay connected on social media sites. Make a "date" with your friends, setting up the next time you are going to talk—even if that means typing rather than literally talking. Don't just say, "Oh, of course we'll stay in touch." Instead, make a plan for how you are actually going to do it. This will help reduce the amount of anxiety you feel about leaving your friends.

Moving is always stressful. If you do feel anxious, remember that your parents or caregivers probably feel even more anxious than you do! It's good to talk about your feelings—it is not weird to be upset, worried, or even mad about having to move. Kids sometimes feel like they should not tell their parents about being upset, because they don't want their parents to feel bad. But an honest conversation could make everybody feel better.

RESEARCH PROJECTS

Prepare a report about homelessness in your community. How many homeless people are there in your city, town, or neighborhood? Find out what services are available; this might include local government, churches, and private charities.

TEXT-DEPENDENT QUESTIONS

1. How many times does an average American move before turning 18?

2. What are some things you can do to reduce anxiety about a move?

3. How many kids experience homelessness in a year?

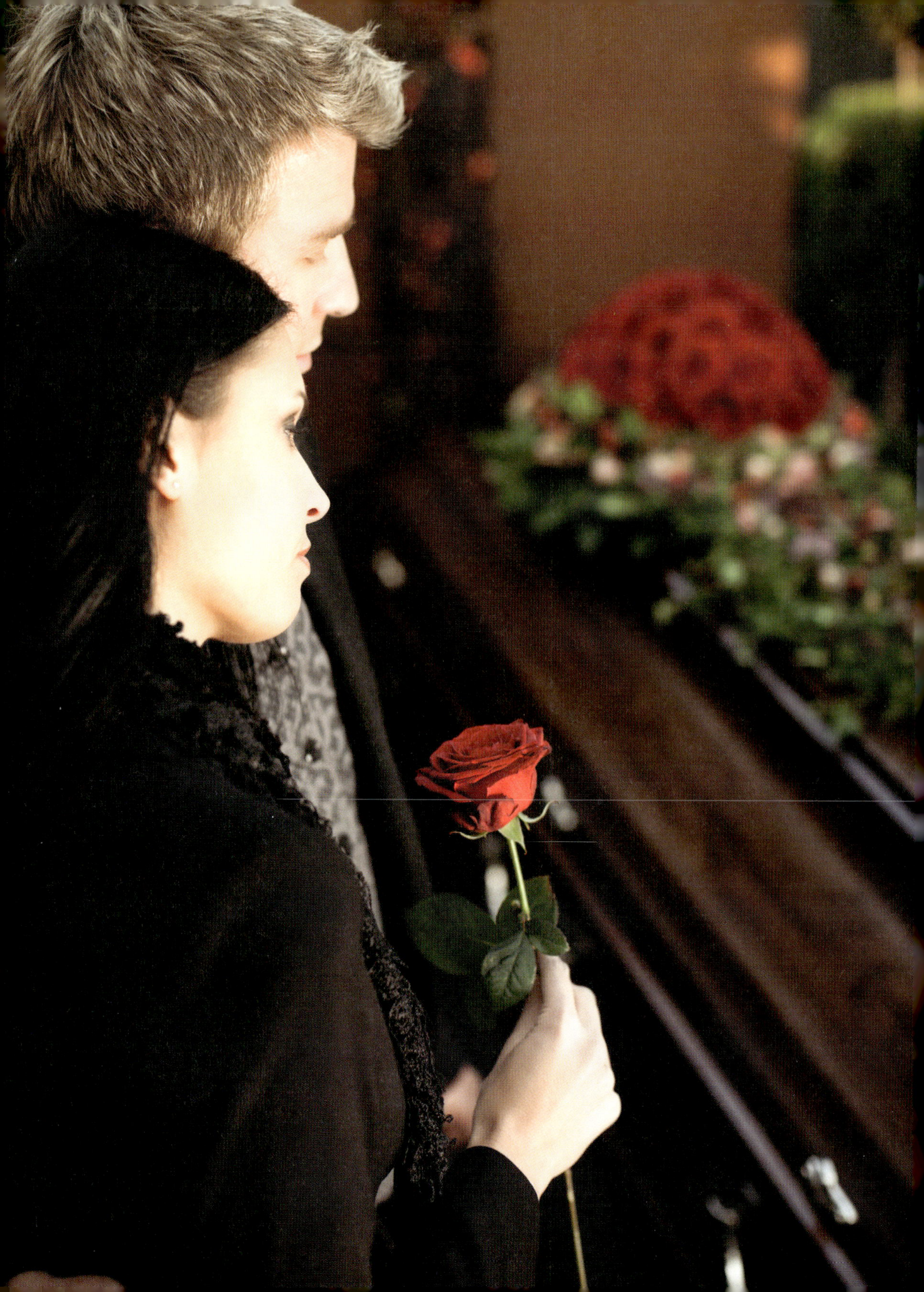

CHAPTER FOUR

DEATH

Imagine that there are aliens out in space and that they are studying our classic stories in order to learn about us. They watch *The Little Mermaid*, *Cinderella*, *Bambi*, *Finding Nemo*, and even *Star Wars.* What impression would the aliens have of families on this planet? Lesson number one would be that, on Earth, motherhood is a death sentence. This is because the "dead mother plot" is extremely common in children's stories.

Fortunately, those stories do not reflect reality. Some kids do lose their parents in tragic ways—due to illness, accident, war, or some other reason. But it is a very uncommon experience. What is *very* common, however, is the fear kids feel that it *could* happen to them. Some kids become extremely fearful about the death of a parent, some other family member (such as a **sibling** or grandparent), or even about their own possible death.

UNDERSTANDING DEATH

Very young kids generally don't worry about their parents getting sick or dying, because they don't

WORDS TO UNDERSTAND

irreversibility: can't be undone or changed.

mortality: the condition of being mortal, or subject to death.

nonfunctionality: the state of not working or operating at all.

sibling: brother or sister.

universality: shared by all members of a particular group.

Most kids can understand what death is by the time they are about six years old.

understand what death even means. They might get upset about being away from their parents. But that is a more vague fear of separation, rather than a specific fear about something bad happening.

People who study childhood development say that kids are usually about four years old before they can begin to understand what death is. Around this age, kids first begin grappling with the idea of **irreversibility**—the idea that certain things can't be undone. Also, kids at this age are paying close attention to what parents say and do. So while they may not quite understand the concept, they do pick up on signals from adults that this thing called death is pretty bad.

But to really understand death, you need to understand two other concepts in addition to

DEATH

THANATOPHOBIA

An extreme fear of death is called *thanatophobia*. The word comes from Thanatos, who was the representation of death in Greek mythology. Thanatos was said to be the son of Nyx (Night) and Erebos (Darkness), and the brother of Hypnos (Sleep). Thanatos also had other siblings, including Geras (Old Age) and Nemesis (Revenge).

Significantly, Thanatos was widely hated by both humans and gods. The ancient Greeks were not any happier about mortality than we are today.

A statue believed to be Thanatos, found at the Temple of Artemis in Ephesos (now part of Turkey).

---

irreversibility. One is **universality**—death happens to everyone eventually, no matter what. And the other is the idea of **nonfunctionality**—that a dead person can't do any of the things living people do and is really truly gone.

It's not until most kids are six or seven years old that they can begin to put all these concepts together in their minds. Of course, particular life events sometimes nudge this understanding along. For example, if a grandparent dies, or if the family dog is hit by a car, a child might start thinking about death sooner than average. But whenever this

EDUCATIONAL VIDEOS

Check out this video that answers some common questions about death.

understanding occurs, the realization that a parent will eventually die is often followed by a fear that it could happen at any moment.

FEARING DEATH

We don't know exactly why some kids feel more-or-less okay with the idea of death—or at least they are able to put it out of their minds—while others feel very anxious and upset by the idea. One factor is temperament. Some people are naturally more anxious than others. Another factor is life circumstances, For example, if a kid experiences the death of a grandparent or pet, that might make him or her more afraid of death in general. Coping with serious illness can also make kids unusually anxious about the possibility of death.

If you are anxious about taking a test, there is something you can do about that anxiety: you can study. Being afraid of death is different, and it can be tough, because there is no action that can "fix" it. Because there is no way to fix a fear of death, people sometimes want to pretend that the fear doesn't exist. But that is often the worst possible strategy. Instead, we need to accept that death is a part of life.

Some kids feel better when they learn more about death as a biological process. In other words, it can help to understand that plants die, animals die, and so on. Just as all living things are born, all of them also die. A 2007 study by researchers

DEATH

in Australia found that the more kids were able to understand death as a biological process, the lower their rates of anxiety became.

As we've said, worrying about death is very common. It's also common to "grow out" of the worry after a while. But sometimes we get stuck in cycles of anxiety, and it can be hard to break those cycles. Kids who are afraid of death often have trouble sleeping. Some might have trouble falling asleep because they keep thinking about their worries, or they may have nightmares about death once they do sleep. They also may be more "clingy," getting upset about having to be separated from their caregivers. They may have trouble paying attention in school because they are too busy

It can be very hard to accept, but death is an inescapable part of life.

FEAR OF ILLNESS

Closely related to the fear of death is the fear of illness. Certainly, anybody who attends school gets exposed to all kinds of germs every day. But although runny noses and sore throats are no fun, they are nothing to be afraid of, either. Unfortunately, not all illnesses are so minor.

Sometimes kids know someone—a parent, sibling, or some other person they're close to—who has a serious illness. This can cause kids to worry that it will happen to them as well. Media coverage of epidemics can also be scary. And even if kids don't follow the news themselves, they may overhear adults discussing world events.

The best way to combat fear of illness is to know the facts. The majority of the scary conditions that adults have are not contagious. You can't catch cancer from being around someone who has it. You won't catch a heart attack from an uncle who had one. Even the disease called AIDS is only contagious in certain, extremely specific situations. Other scary diseases, such as Ebola, are extremely rare in North America. You may hear about them in the media, but you are not going to see them in your neighborhood.

Second, in the majority of cases, people who get sick also get well. It may take time for them to recover. And in some situations, the illness may not go away completely. But our medical knowledge is more sophisticated today than at any point in human history.

So, yes, there is always a chance that you or someone you love could become ill. But that chance is actually pretty small. And if it does happen, doctors can probably do a lot to help.

DEATH

worrying about whether their caregivers are safe. If an intense anxiety about death is interfering with your ability to sleep, concentrate, or simply have fun, you should ask adults you trust for help.

THE HUMAN EXPERIENCE

It's important to understand that fearing death is not only a common experience, but it is also uniquely human. Animals don't fear death, because they don't understand the concept in the first place. Some people say that an awareness of our **mortality** is precisely what makes us different from the rest of the animal kingdom. And a great many works of art have been created by people struggling with exactly these issues. So if you are worried about death, you are definitely not alone.

Death is part of a cycle—people are born, they grow, they become old, and then they die. Our human awareness that life can end is, philosophers say, exactly what makes life so precious. Death reminds us to make the most of the time we have.

RESEARCH PROJECT

Choose a culture that's different from your own and find out about what that culture believes about death. You could choose a culture from history (such as ancient Egypt or Rome), a religion that is not your own (such as Buddhism or Islam), or a modern culture you don't know much about (such as an indigenous group). What beliefs do people from that culture hold about the meaning of death? Do they believe in an afterlife?

TEXT-DEPENDENT QUESTIONS

1. Roughly how old are most kids when they begin to understand death?
2. What are the three concepts related to understanding death?
3. What are some things you can do to cope with an intense fear of death?

FURTHER READING

Arkowitz, Hal, and Scott O. Lilenfeld. "Is Divorce Bad for Children?" *Scientific American*, March 1, 2013. https://www.scientificamerican.com/article/is-divorce-bad-for-children/.

Bassuk, Ellen L., Carmela J. DeCandia, Corey Anne Beach, and Fred Berman. *America's Youngest Outcasts: A Report Card on Child Homelessness*. American Institutes for Research, November 2014. http://www.air.org/sites/default/files/downloads/report/Americas-Youngest-Outcasts-Child-Homelessness-Nov2014.pdf.

Darling, Nancy. "Moving Is Tough for Kids." *Psychology Today*, July 11, 2010. https://www.psychologytoday.com/blog/thinking-about-kids/201007/moving-is-tough-kids.

Ehmke, Rachel. "Helping Children Deal with Grief." Child Mind Institute. http://childmind.org/article/helping-children-deal-grief/.

Hughes, Lynn B. *You Are Not Alone: Teens Talk about Life after the Loss of a Parent*. New York: Scholastic, 2005.

Stueit, Trudi Strain. *Surviving Divorce: Teens Talk about What Hurts and What Helps*. New York: Scholastic, 2007.

EDUCATIONAL VIDEOS

Chapter One: John P. Cordray. "How to Deal with Anxiety and Family Conflict." https://youtu.be/4UXCam6of0Q.

Chapter Two: Christina McGhee. "SPLIT: A Film about Divorce for Children and Their Parents." https://youtu.be/SziFKfIlloQ.

Chapter Three: Reagan Gresh. "Survive Moving & 'Being the New Kid.'" https://youtu.be/sX2OQunWZ5g.

Chapter Four: Ask a Mortician. "Death Questions from Kids!" https://youtu.be/LUpMPAiyHkI.

SERIES GLOSSARY

adaptive: a helpful response to a particular situation.

bias: a feeling against a particular thing or idea.

biofeedback: monitoring of bodily functions with the goal of learning to control those functions.

cognitive: relating to the brain and thought.

comorbid: when one illness or disorder is present alongside another one.

context: the larger situation in which an event takes place.

diagnose: to identify an illness or disorder.

exposure: having contact with something.

extrovert: a person who enjoys being with others.

harassment: picking on another person frequently and deliberately.

hypnosis: creating a state of consciousness where someone is awake but highly open to suggestion.

inhibitions: feelings that restricts what we do or say.

introvert: a person who prefers being alone.

irrational: baseless; something that's not connected to reality.

melatonin: a substance that helps the body regulate sleep.

milestone: an event that marks a stage in development.

motivating: something that makes you want to work harder.

occasional: from time to time; not often.

panic attack: sudden episode of intense, overwhelming fear.

paralyzing: something that makes you unable to move (can refer to physical movement as well as emotions).

peers: people who are roughly the same age as you.

perception: what we see and believe to be true.

persistent: continuing for a noticeable period.

phobia: extreme fear of a particular thing.

preventive: keeping something from happening.

probability: the likelihood that a particular thing will happen.

psychological: having to do with the mind and thoughts.

rational: based on a calm understanding of facts, rather than emotion.

sedative: a type of drug that slows down bodily processes, making people feel relaxed or even sleepy.

self-conscious: overly aware of yourself, to the point that it makes you awkward.

serotonin: a chemical in the brain that is important in moods.

stereotype: an oversimplified idea about a type of person that may not be true for any given individual.

stigma: a sense of shame or disgrace associated with a particular state of being.

stimulant: a group of substances that speed up bodily processes.

subconscious: thoughts and feelings you have but may not be aware of.

syndrome: a condition.

treatable: describes a medical condition that can be healed.

upheaval: a period of great change or uncertainty.

INDEX

counseling   26
custody   15, 17, 18–19, 25, 26, 27
"dead mother plot"   37
death
   as biological process   40–41
   fear of   40–41, 43
   irreversibility and   38
   understanding concept of   37–39, 43
   universality and   39
deployment   9, 11, 17
deportation   9, 11
divorce   10, 11
   "no-fault"   20
   defined   15–16
   fear of   20–24
   first year after   25
   long-term effects of   26–27
   rates of   20
domestic abuse   21

family
   talking to   22–24, 35
   types of fears   11
foster care   13
grandparents   12–13, 37, 39, 40
homelessness   31
illness, fear of   40, 42
marriage   15–16
moving, advice about   32–35
moving
   numbers of Americans   29
   reasons for   29–30, 31
   staying friends after   34–35
National Child Abuse Hotline   21
National Sexual Assault Hotline   21
separation   17
Thanatos   39
visitation   19

ABOUT THE ADVISOR

Anne S. Walters is Clinical Associate Professor of Psychiatry and Human Behavior at the Alpert Medical School of Brown University. She is also Chief Psychologist for Bradley Hospital. She is actively involved in teaching activities within the Clinical Psychology Training Programs of the Alpert Medical School and serves as Child Track Seminar Co-Coordinator. Dr. Walters completed her undergraduate work at Duke University, graduate school at Georgia State University, internship at UTexas Health Science Center, and postdoctoral fellowship at Brown University.

ABOUT THE AUTHOR

H. W. Poole is a writer and editor of books for young people, including the sets, *Families Today* and *Mental Illnesses and Disorders: Awareness and Understanding* (Mason Crest). She created the *Horrors of History* series (Charlesbridge) and the *Ecosystems* series (Facts On File). She has also been responsible for many critically acclaimed reference books, including *Political Handbook of the World* (CQ Press) and the *Encyclopedia of Terrorism* (SAGE). She was coauthor and editor of *The History of the Internet* (ABC-CLIO), which won the 2000 American Library Association RUSA award.

PHOTO CREDITS

Cover (clockwise): iStock/kzenon; Shutterstock/Ampyang; iStock/kali9; iStock/TatyanaGl
iStock: 8 Feverpitched; 10 Wavebreakmedia; 11 Anna Bryukhanova ; 12 Geber86; 14 TatyanaGl; 16 castenoid; 17 MivPiv; 19 PeopleImages; 22 PeopleImages; 24 ClarkandCompany; 26 izusek; 28 kali9; 30 monkeybusinessimages; 33 DGLimages; 34 gemphotography; 36 kzenon; 38 RichLegg; 41 mactrunk
Wikimedia: 39 Marie-Lan Nguyen